Effective decision-making

Effective decision-making

A self-development programme

Bryan D Prescott

Gower

Published by Gower Publishing Company Limited,
Gower House, Croft Road, Aldershot, Hants GU11 3HR
Reprinted 1985

British Library Cataloguing in Publication Data

Prescott, Bryan D
    Effective decision-making.
    1. Decision-making
    I. Title
    658.4'03   HD30.23

    ISBN 0-566-02211-7 Pbk

Typeset by Pintail Studios Ltd, Ringwood, Hampshire
Printed and bound in Great Britain by
Antony Rowe Ltd, Chippenham, Wilts

Contents

Preface

Many managers tend to adopt a particular decision-making
process and apply it with little variation to all situations.
Others, a minority, use a range of decision-making processes.
Faced with a similar or even the same problem different
managers employ different decision-making processes,
some preferring an autocratic approach while others use
varying degrees of participation or delegation. These
observations, based on my knowledge of a large number of
managers over a period of 25 years, raised two major
questions. Firstly, is a particular decision-making process
more effective in a given situation or is the choice of process
unimportant? Secondly, if some decision-making
processes are more effective than others, can they be
identified in advance for different situations? To answer the
first question it was crucial to define 'effective decision-
making', and this presented a serious problem. After much
thought and many modifications an acceptable definition
was formulated. The second question was partly solved by
Dr Victor H Vroom of Yale University and Dr Phillip W
Yetton of Manchester Business School, in their book
Leadership and Decision-Making (University of Pittsburgh
Press, 1973). They developed a model for selecting decision-
making processes in different situations. However, this model

did not include negotiation, which is an important and
widely used decision-making process.

It appeared to me that there was a great need at all levels
of management for training in decision-making skills.
I decided that a self-development programme offered the
best way of meeting this need, for the following reasons:

1. It could reach a large target population
2. It could overcome the growing problem of releasing
    managers to attend off-the-job courses
3. It would enable managers to study in their own time
    and at their own pace
4. It would provide guided practice and feedback on
    performance, both of which are necessary for skill
    development.

Having created the self-development programme, the next
problem was how to validate it. This was dealt with in two
ways. Firstly, a number of leaders — headmasters, research
officers, management tutors, managers, supervisors and union
officials — read it and gave their comments. Secondly,
I designed, developed and implemented a decision-making
course for middle and senior managers. The validation process
confirmed the great need at all levels for such training and
proved the relevance of the self-development programme to
anybody having to make decisions, especially managers who
have to consider the needs and aspirations of other people.
It should also be of value to training specialists and to
students of management.

This book highlights the need to take account of the
situation variables before making a decision; it shows that in
some cases it is appropriate to decide autocratically, while in
others varying degrees of participation or delegation will be
more effective. But, most important of all, it demonstrates
that decision-making skills can be developed in a systematic
manner.

I wish to acknowledge the opportunity afforded to me by
the Iron and Steel Industry Training Board to implement and

validate the decision-making course. I would also like to thank the training staff of the British Steel Corporation's Llanwern and Port Talbot works who sat through the pilot courses and provided me with valuable feedback and ideas which have been incorporated in the programme.

I wish to thank my colleagues, Mr Arwyn Reynolds, Mr John Davies and Mr Bryan Edwards for their help and many suggestions and, finally, Dorothy, Sheridan, Nigel, Elaine and Melonie for their support and encouragement.

Bryan D Prescott

1   *Introduction*

If you occupy a leadership position such that you supervise others and make decisions, you should be able to answer the following questions:

1. What is an effective decision?
2. When should you involve others in the decision-making process and why?
3. What criteria can be used to select a decision-making process which is most likely to generate an effective decision?

Do not be alarmed if you are unable to answer all of the above questions — you have something in common with most other leaders in that you almost certainly have not been trained to make effective decisions. Even very experienced managers have difficulty defining an effective decision; and when asked to explain why they consult with subordinates in making some decisions but not others, they are rarely able to provide rational and consistent reasons — it is usually a highly subjective process, even an intuitive one. That is not to say that leaders who use an intuitive approach to the selection of a decision-making process never make effective decisions: in fact, they often do. The problem is: how do you train someone to select a decision-making process designed to generate an effective decision based on the use of intuition?

Decision-making courses often teach a number of techniques such as the problem-solving approach, simulation or creative thinking but rarely provide guidelines about the decision-making processes which should be used in different situations. That is, should I solve the problem alone, consult with others, delegate the problem to my subordinate or negotiate a solution which is acceptable to all concerned? It is probably the lack of criteria on which decision-making process to use in a given situation that has inhibited training provision in this vital leadership skill.

That decision-making is a key leadership skill is generally accepted and leaders who make bad decisions usually suffer the consequences of their actions. Thus, we hear frequently of football team managers being dismissed because their team is performing badly. The manager is blamed for having made poor decisions which cost the club large sums of money in falling gates and the purchase of players. Similarly in politics, if policies fail the consequences are electoral defeat. If a manager in industry makes poor decisions, the results are reflected in low output, off-grade material, excessive down-time and industrial relations problems.

In the immediate past, leadership style was mainly autocratic — the extreme example of this being the so called 'iron-masters' who not only controlled their employees in an autocratic manner at work, but exercised considerable control over their social lives as well. As political, economic and social changes have taken place, particularly the establishment of effective trade unions, it has become increasingly more difficult to make decisions in isolation from those affected by them. There is growing pressure on leaders to consult in varying degrees with other interested parties.

This raises questions about the relationship between leadership style, the task to be performed and the generation of effective decisions. For example, is the autocratic style still relevant? If so, under what circumstances should it be applied? When is it necessary to consult with others and why? What degree of consultation is necessary? And finally, what is an effective decision?

Unfortunately, leaders often make decisions on the basis of fixed attitudes, partial knowledge, prejudice, or allegiance to a particular dogma rather than an objective analysis which takes account of all the relevant factors. A basic problem for most leaders is that they lack guidelines which enable them consistently to generate effective decisions.

This self-development programme provides answers to the above questions. It has deliberately been kept concise so that leaders can work through it in about two to three hours of study. It concentrates on principles, definitions and case studies which allow leaders to practise and develop the skill of selecting decision-making processes which are most likely to generate effective decisions.

On completion of this programme you will be able to:

(a) define an effective decision;
(b) name five decision-making processes;
(c) analyse in terms of seven diagnostic questions any situation requiring a decision;
(d) select the appropriate decision-making process;
(e) determine the appropriate degree of participation of others in the decision-making process.

2 Effective decision-making

Effective decision-making enables leaders to analyse a situation requiring a decision and from that analysis to select the decision-making process which is most likely to generate an effective decision (ED).

Five distinct decision-making processes may be identified. They are:

Autocratic
Autocratic (information- or skill-seeking)
Consultation
Negotiation
Delegation

Take, for example, a manager who has to decide whether or not to introduce trained operator instructors. There are three reasons why he faces this problem. First, serious operational problems have been shown to be the result of traditional on-the-job training (i.e. training alongside an experienced operator who has not been trained as an instructor). Second, there is pressure from the Industry Training Board to introduce trained instructors — failure to comply could lead to liability for levy. Third, there is

pressure arising from the requirements of the Health and
Safety at Work Act to provide adequate instruction, training
and information. The manager is likely to meet opposition
from experienced operatives on the shopfloor who may see
the introduction of trained instructors as a reflection of
management's lack of confidence in their ability. There are
also the problems of selection and training, apart from the
cost of introducing the scheme.

In such a situation the manager could make an *autocratic*
decision based on his knowledge of the situation and simply
decree that trained instructors will be introduced. He could
seek information from others, evaluate it and then make an
autocratic decision; he could *consult* with all interested
parties, evaluate their suggested solutions and then make a
decision which may or may not take account of their
opinions; he could *negotiate* with interested parties and reach
a compromise solution which is acceptable to all parties; or,
finally, he could *delegate* the problem to an individual or
group and give them the responsibility for the decision.

Effective decision-making offers an approach that enables
a leader faced with such a problem to select the process most
likely to generate an effective decision. It does so by requiring
him to analyse the situation by giving a yes/no answer to a
series of questions and then applying that analysis to a
standard network designed to indicate the appropriate
decision-making process. (The network itself is presented in
Chapter 6, together with a full explanation of the required
analysis.)

If the analysis is applied to the situation just described,
the network leads to 'negotiation'. In other words, it indicates
that the manager should negotiate a solution acceptable to all
the parties concerned. The analysis predicts that negotiation
is the most likely way to produce an effective decision.

3 Effective decisions

What is an effective decision? This question is perhaps best answered by considering those factors which influence the effectiveness of decisions. There is, firstly, the degree to which the *aim* of the decision is achieved. Thus, if the aim is to increase production by at least 10 per cent, then three possible decisions may vary in the degree to which they achieve that aim. For example, suppose that the three decisions are:

(a) Introduce overtime working
(b) Recruit temporary labour
(c) Introduce new technology.

It might well be that (c) is expected to increase production by 20 per cent, (b) by 12 per cent and (a) by 10 per cent.

Another important factor is the *cost* of implementing the decision. For example, the cost of (c) may be £250,000, the cost of (b) £60,000 and the cost of (a) £80,000. A third factor is the *time* taken to implement the decision. Thus, (c) might take nine months, (b) might take three months, since there is the problem of recruiting and training temporary labour, whereas (a) could be implemented immediately.

If time is the critical factor then decision (a) is the highest quality decision. If cost is the critical factor then the highest quality decision is (b), and if increase in output is

more critical than time or cost, the choice must be (c).
Note that in the long term decision (c) might also be the
most cost effective. In practice, the quality of a decision is
often a balance between the relative importance of the three
factors, aim, cost and time.

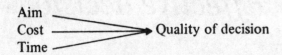

Another important factor is the *acceptability* of the
decision. For example, suppose that solutions in order of
quality are (c), (b) and (a), but that the men affected by the
decisions prefer them in the order (a), (b) and (c). They may
want to work overtime, they may be reluctant or even refuse
to work with temporary labour and they may fear new
technology because of possible job losses. Failure to take
account of these fears could mean that implementation of
the highest quality decision (c) fails to be fully effective
because of the men's refusal to co-operate. The quality of a
decision cannot therefore be treated in isolation from those
affected by the decision or from those who have to
implement it.

To summarise, the factors influencing the effectiveness of
a decision are:

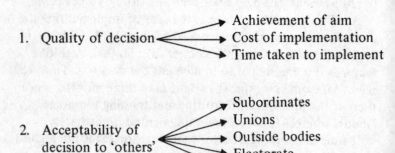

The word 'others' refers to anyone who is either affected by the decision or has to implement it. Consider the manager, discussed earlier, who had to make a decision about trained instructors for operative training. Apart from the quality of the decision, he also has to assess the acceptability of his decision to the men on the shopfloor, to the appropriate industry training board and to the safety inspectorate.

Leaders often tend to select decisions of the highest quality — achievement of aim, at minimum cost in the shortest time — without fully assessing the consequences of the decision on 'others'. The result is that the decision often fails to be effective because 'others' refuse to co-operate or, in the extreme case, resort to work-to-rule or strike action.

We are now in a position to define an effective decision. There are four cases to consider:

1. If the quality of the decision is critical and acceptability is also critical, then the effective decision (ED) is the highest quality decision which is acceptable to others. This may be expressed as:

$$ED = Q_{max} Acc$$

For example, the manager discussed previously who wants to increase production by 10 per cent considered:

(a) asking the men to work overtime;
(b) recruiting temporary labour;
(c) introducing new technology.

The quality of his decision is obviously important in terms of cost, time and achievement of aim. There is also likely to be an acceptability problem since the men may refuse to work overtime, work with temporary labour or co-operate with management on the introduction of new technology which might create redundancies. In this case, the effective decision is the highest quality decision which is acceptable.

2. If the quality of the decision is critical and
    acceptability is not a problem, then the effective
    decision is the highest quality decision. This may be
    expressed as:

$$ED = Q_{max}$$

Consider an engineer who has to schedule materials and
equipment for a development project. He has to ensure that
the materials arrive in time for the work to start on schedule,
but not so soon that they will be lying around for long
periods. In this case, the effective decision is the highest
quality decision since there is no acceptability factor involved.
The engineer does not need the support or active co-operation
of others to implement his decision effectively.

3. If the quality of the decision is not important but
    acceptability is critical, then the effective decision is
    the one which is most acceptable. This may be
    expressed as:

$$ED = Acc_{max}$$

An office supervisor has to decide which of six typists are
to receive four new electric typewriters. All of the typists are
competent and there is little difference in seniority. In this
case there is no quality requirement, and from the
supervisor's point of view it does not matter who receives the
typewriters. There is an acceptability problem, however, since
all of the typists would prefer to have one of the new
machines. In this case the effective decision is clearly the one
which is most acceptable to the typists.

4. If neither the quality nor the acceptability factor is
    important, then any decision is likely to be effective.
    One can literally toss a coin to make the decision.
    This may be expressed as:

$$ED = any\ decision$$

A manager has to decide between three tenders to paint an

office block. The three contractors concerned are all reliable and respectable concerns, capable of performing the task satisfactorily. The difference in the quoted prices is insignificant in comparison to the total cost. In this case there is no quality requirement, since they can all perform the task to the required standard (aim) and there is no significant cost or time difference. There is also no acceptability requirement — the manager does not need the co-operation or support of others to make the decision. The effective decision is, therefore, any decision.

Summary

The factors influencing the effectiveness of a decision are the quality of the decision — aim, cost and time — and its acceptability to those responsible for implementing it or affected by it.

The effective decision in a particular situation depends on the relative importance of the quality and acceptability factors. The four cases are:

$$ED = Q_{max} \; Acc$$

$$ED = Q_{max}$$

$$ED = Acc_{max}$$

$$ED = any \; decision$$

4 *Decision-making processes*

In Chapter 2 we identified five decision-making processes.
These may be designated by the letters A, I, C, N and D,
as follows:

      A = Autocratic
      I = Autocratic (information- or skill-seeking)
      C = Consultation
      N = Negotiation
      D = Delegation

Let us consider each of these processes in turn:

Autocratic – A

In this case, the leader solves the problem using the
information which he possesses. He does not consult with
anyone else or seek information from other sources.
It assumes that the leader has sufficient information and
skill to generate high quality decisions.

Autocratic (information- or skill-seeking) – I

The leader does not possess sufficient information or skill to
make an effective decision. He therefore has to obtain (from

others) the information or skill which will enable him to
generate a high quality decision. He may or may not tell
others what the problem is — usually he simply asks for
information. The leader then evaluates the information and
makes a decision. This is a variation of the autocratic process.

Consultation — C

The leader explains the situation to the group or individual
whom he provides with relevant information, and together
they generate and evaluate solutions. Alternatively he may
ask either the group or the individual to conduct a survey/
investigation and make recommendations. Finally, the leader
evaluates the solutions or recommendations which the group
or individual has put forward and then makes a decision
which may or may not take these views into account.

Negotiation — N

The leader explains the situation to the group/individual and
provides the relevant information. Together they attempt to
reconcile differences and negotiate a solution which is
acceptable to all parties. The leader may consult with others
before the meeting in order to prepare his case and generate
alternative decisions which are acceptable to him.

Delegation — D

Responsibility and authority for making the decision are
given to the group/individual. The leader provides all the
relevant information which he possesses. The leader's role is
very much like that of a chairman. He guides and controls
the discussion but does not attempt to force his opinions on

Table 4.1 *Participation in decision-making processes*

Leader-centred ⟶   ⟵ Group-centred

	A	I	C	N	D
Participants	Leader	Leader and others	Leader and others	Leader and others	Leader and others
Role of participants	Leader generates and evaluates solution alone	Others provide leader with skill or information, then as A	Others generate solutions or make recommendations	Others negotiate a solution with leader	Group generates, evaluates and makes decision
Who makes the decision	Leader	Leader	Leader	Leader and group together	Group

the group. He is prepared to accept and implement any solution proposed by the group/individual.

As can be seen from Table 4.1, as one moves from process A to process D the extent of the participation increases until in D the group/individual actually makes the decision.

5 Selection of decision-making processes

Read the following six case studies and select the decision-making process from A, I, C, N and D, which you think is most likely to generate an effective decision in each case. There are two reasons for doing this exercise. Firstly it will enable you to compare and contrast your selections with those in Chapter 7 later on and, secondly, it will provide you with feedback on your present leadership style.

Case study 1

You are the manager of a small television, radio and
electronics business and for some time you have had
complaints from your salesgirls and counter-girls about the
need to redecorate the large shop in which they work.
You recently agreed to do this and you have received three
tenders from reliable and well-known local contractors.
They are all capable of doing the work to the required
standard and there is little difference in the quoted costs or
times for the job.

  You recently asked your employees for their suggestions
on suitable colour schemes and there was considerable
difference of opinion. You now have to decide which tender
to accept.

Case study 2

You are an engineer in charge of the commissioning of a chemical plant and it is necessary for you to estimate the rate of progress of the various stages of the work in order to schedule the materials and equipment required. You are familiar with the work in hand and possess all the necessary information about the materials and equipment required. With this information it is possible to estimate the times at which materials and equipment will be required at the various commissioning stages. It is very important that your estimates are accurate since if materials are not available at the right time work will be held up. Equally, if materials and equipment arrive too soon they will be lying around idle. Your commissioning team are all committed to the plant being commissioned on time.

Case study 3

You are a training manager employed by a firm of consultants and you have to select three of your eight training advisers to work on an assignment abroad. The assignment involves a training needs analysis, preparation of training programmes and the training of local instructors.

The assignment is expected to last about six months and is in a remote part of the Middle East with poor facilities and a ban on the consumption of alcohol. Your advisers are all experienced personnel and each of them is capable of performing the task satisfactorily.

Case study 4

You are a project leader and your main objective is to commission a new plant, line 2, on time without adversely affecting production on the existing plant, line 1.

Most of the operatives working on line 1 want to transfer to line 2 because it is expected that working conditions will be much better on the new line and the rates of pay higher. Senior operatives working on line 1 expect to be given preference over less senior ones and all of the operatives on line 1 expect to be given preference over operatives working in other departments of the works.

You, however, want to transfer only the best operatives from line 1 to line 2 and make up the balance with operatives from other departments. Your reason for wanting to do this is that the speed of operation on line 2 will be significantly faster than on line 1. This means that operatives working on line 2 will need to be much more skilled at fault rectification than those working on line 1. The ability to react quickly to control panel and video display unit (VDU) cues is essential.

Case study 5

A company owns three factories — at Port Talbot, Redcar
and Sheffield — all of which produce the same product.
Production from these factories is distributed via three warehouses located in Birmingham, Dagenham and Oxford.
At the moment the total demand from the three warehouses
is equal to the total capacity of the factories:

Factory	Capacity (tons per month)	Warehouse	Demand (tons per month)
Port Talbot	3,000	Birmingham	6,000
Redcar	5,000	Dagenham	3,000
Sheffield	6,000	Oxford	5,000
	14,000		14,000

You are based at head office and you have to decide on
the pattern of distribution from the factories to the warehouses. The pattern is changed from time to time as a result
of complaints from the factory and warehouse managers
about the allocation of transport costs. The total cost of
distribution therefore varies from time to time. The transport
costs (in £ per ton) for delivering from each factory to each
warehouse are as follows:

	Birmingham	Dagenham	Oxford
Port Talbot	3	7	4
Redcar	6	10	9
Sheffield	4	9	6

You are naturally concerned to keep transport costs to a
minimum from the company point of view, whereas each
works manager wants to keep his own costs to a minimum.
There is therefore often a clash of interests between you and
the works managers.

Case study 6

You are based at divisional headquarters and work on a range of problems as a trouble-shooter. You have been given the task of developing a quality control recording system to be used in each of the twelve works in the division.

There have been numerous complaints about the lack of common terminology and the use of words peculiar to specific works which complicate the processing of the data. Also, methods used to record data vary between works and the accuracy of some of the data is regarded as suspect. The variations in practice could complicate the establishment of a system common to all works. You possess information on the different terminologies being used but you have no information on local practices for recording the data.

Both division and the works would benefit from a standardised system which would improve the accuracy of the information, since important quality control and quality assurance decisions are based on the data provided by the works.

Successful implementation of a common recording system will require the active co-operation and commitment of the works quality control staff. Care will be needed in handling the situation since although they all stand to benefit from an improved system, they may resent what they regard as divisional interference in works operating procedure.

6 Criteria for selecting decision-making processes

Let us now examine in detail the method used in effective decision-making to select the process most likely to generate an effective decision. This is done in two stages, as outlined in Chapter 2. The situation requiring a decision is first of all analysed by answering Yes or No to seven diagnostic questions. These questions are designed to determine the relative importance of the quality and acceptability factors of the decision and the influence of participation by 'others' on those factors.

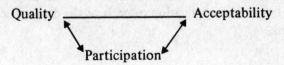

Quality ———————— Acceptability

Participation

The questions are as follows:

1. Are decisions likely to differ significantly in their quality (aim, cost, time)?
2. Can I make a high quality decision without the aid of others?

3. Do I know what aid is required and how to obtain it?
4. Do I need the acceptance of others to implement my decision?
5. Are others likely to accept my decision without being involved in making the decision?
6. Do others share the same aims that I want to achieve in making the decision?
7. Are others, if consulted, likely to accept my decision?

Thus a certain situation requiring a decision to be made may be analysed, for example, as follows:

$$
\begin{aligned}
1 &= \text{Yes} \\
2 &= \text{No} \\
3 &= \text{Yes} \\
4 &= \text{Yes} \\
5 &= \text{No} \\
6 &= \text{Yes} \\
7 &= \text{No}
\end{aligned}
$$

The analysis is then applied to the decision network shown on pp. 28 and 29. In this case it leads to decision-making processes C (consultation) or D (delegation). In certain cases some questions may not apply: the network is constructed in such a way that it will by-pass questions which do not apply to a particular problem situation. (The logic of the decision network is explained fully in the Appendix.)

It is now necessary to consider in some detail the interpretation and application of each of the diagnostic questions.

See the decision network, overleaf.

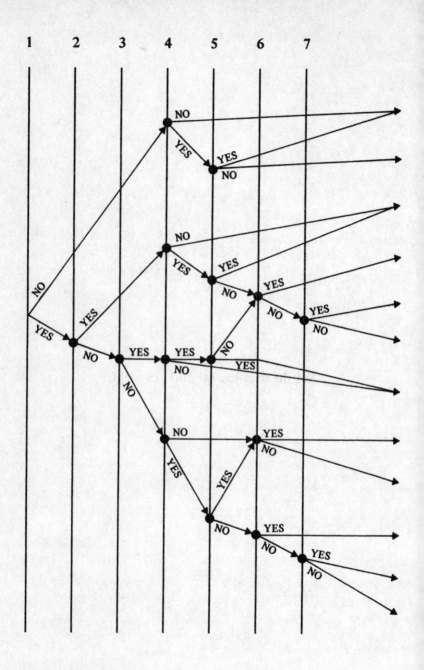

The decision network

Decision-making process	Effective decision
A	*Any decision*
D	Acc_{max}
A or I or C	Q_{max}
C or D	$Q_{max} Acc$
C	$Q_{max} Acc$
N	$Q_{max} Acc$
I or C	$Q_{max} Acc$
C or D	Q_{max}
C	$Q_{max} Acc$
C or D	$Q_{max} Acc$
C	$Q_{max} Acc$
N	$Q_{max} Acc$

KEY:

A	Autocratic
I	Autocratic (information- or skill-seeking)
C	Consultation
N	Negotiation
D	Delegation
Q	Quality
Acc	Acceptability

Question 1
Are decisions likely to differ significantly in their quality (aim, cost, time)?

The point to grasp here is that it is the extent to which solutions differ in their quality rather than the quality of the decision itself which is important. For example, consider the manager in Case Study 1 who has to decide which tender to accept. In this case, Question 1 would be answered No since the decisions do not vary significantly in quality. All three contractors are competent to achieve the aim and there is little difference in the cost or time factors.

Consider the office supervisor in Chapter 3 who has to decide which of the typists are to receive the four new electric typewriters. Question 1 would again be answered No since it does not matter to the supervisor who receives the typewriters − they are all competent to use them and there are no cost or time factors involved.

Consider a marketing manager who has to make a decision on the pricing of a product in a highly competitive market. If the price is set too high there may be a failure to win the required orders and large stocks will result. On the other hand, if the price is set too low, customer orders are not likely to be met. Both results are undesirable and costly to the firm. Question 1 would therefore be answered Yes since solutions could differ markedly in their quality.

Consider the manager in Case Study 5 who has to decide on the distribution of output to the warehouses. The aim is obviously to keep transport costs to a minimum. This problem may be solved by a process of trial and error illustrated in Figs. 6.1 and 6.2. In the first example transport costs are shown to be £90,000, which represents the maximum cost solution.

Warehouse demand

Factory capacity		Birmingham 6,000 tons	Dagenham 3,000	Oxford 5,000	
Port Talbot 3,000		3 3,000	7	4	£/ton
Redcar 5,000		6 3,000	10	9 2,000	
Sheffield 6,000		4	9 3,000	6 3,000	

Fig. 6.1   *Maximum cost solution*

In Fig. 6.1 we have:

$$3,000 \times 3 = £9,000$$
$$3,000 \times 6 = £18,000$$
$$3,000 \times 9 = £27,000$$
$$2,000 \times 9 = £18,000$$
$$3,000 \times 6 = £18,000$$

Total transport costs = £90,000

Before referring to Fig. 6.2, which indicates the minimum cost solution, see if you can work it out yourself.

Figure 6.2, Minimum cost solution, is overleaf.

Warehouse demand

Factory capacity	Birmingham 6,000 tons	Dagenham 3,000	Oxford 5,000	
Port Talbot 3,000	3	7	4 3,000	£/ton
Redcar 5,000	6 2,000	10 3,000	9	
Sheffield 6,000	4 4,000	9	6 2,000	

Fig. 6.2   *Minimum cost solution*

In Fig. 6.2 we have:

$$
\begin{aligned}
3{,}000 \times 4 &= £12{,}000 \\
2{,}000 \times 6 &= £12{,}000 \\
3{,}000 \times 10 &= £30{,}000 \\
4{,}000 \times 4 &= £16{,}000 \\
2{,}000 \times 6 &= £12{,}000 \\
\end{aligned}
$$

Total transport costs = £82,000

It is possible to generate a range of solutions between £82,000 and £90,000. Clearly the answer to Question 1 is Yes since decisions vary significantly in their cost — by as much as £8,000 per month.

Consider the following aim: to increase production by 10 per cent. Suppose there are four possible decisions as shown below:

Decision	Achievement of aim	Cost	Time to implement decision
A	10%	£8,000	3 months
B	10%	£9,000	5 months
C	8%	£7,800	5 months
D	7%	£7,500	3 months

Clearly, the decisions vary in their quality and since decision A is expected to increase production by 10 per cent at a cost of £8,000 in three months it is the highest quality decision.

Thus, if some solutions are likely to be better than others to the extent that they are more effective in achieving the aim, less costly or take less time — answer Yes to Question 1 and move on to Question 2. If solutions are not likely to vary significantly, or at all, in terms of cost, time or achievement of aim, answer No. If you answer No to Question 1, Questions 2 and 3 are not applicable.

Question 2
Can I make a high quality decision without the aid of others?

This question is designed to protect the quality of the
decision, since if the leader does not possess sufficient
information or skill to generate a high quality decision, he
should not use the A leadership style. The manager in Case
Study 5 knows the demands from the warehouses, capacities
from the works and the costs of transportation. He therefore
possesses sufficient information to generate a high quality
decision; thus, Question 2 would be answered Yes.
Unfortunately, leaders sometimes assume that they possess
the necessary information when in fact they do not.
They therefore make autocratic A decisions which fail to be
fully effective. This weakness represents another powerful
reason for leaders to receive formal training in decision-
making skills. At least, they will then be aware of the dangers
and be more likely to appraise the relevance of their
knowledge and information critically before deciding to
make an autocratic decision.

Serious operational problems such as poor output,
excessive delay on machines, off-grade material and accidents
are sometimes the result of management's failure to realise
the serious drawbacks of 'Nellie' instruction (instruction by
an experienced worker who has not been trained as an
instructor), which can result in skill and knowledge
deficiencies.[1] Now consider the position of the manager
discussed earlier who had to decide whether to retain the
existing on-the-job training arrangements or to introduce
trained instructors. The chances are that he does not possess
sufficient information to generate a high quality decision.
For example, he needs to know:

(a) the cost of the existing system;
(b) the deficiencies of the existing system;

1. 'The Trouble Shooting Approach to Training', Industrial and Commercial
   Training 1975 Vol. 7, no. 1.

   (c) the advantages of using trained instructors;
   (d) the cost of introducing the proposed system.

He would almost certainly need to consult with others before being able to generate an effective decision. Question 2 would thus be answered No.

Question 3
Do I know what aid is required and how to obtain it?

This question is also designed to protect the quality of the decision and assess the degree to which others need be involved in the decision-making process. For example, you may require additional information or the services of a skilled person. You may, for instance, need someone to do a critical path analysis, simulation exercise or sensitivity analysis to assist you to make high quality decisions. You only answer Yes to this question if you are able to answer Yes to both parts of it, that is:

Do I know what aid is required?
Do I know how to obtain it?

Consider again Case Study 5. Suppose that one of the works managers had been asked to generate a minimum cost solution for the company overall rather than for his own works. That manager would answer No to Question 2 since he would not know the outputs or transport costs for the other works. He would, however, know exactly what information was required — factory outputs, transport costs and warehouse demands — and where to obtain it. Question 3 would therefore be answered Yes. In general, if the problem or situation is a structured one, i.e. if there is a laid-down procedure for dealing with it or the variables and data required to solve it are known, then the question is answered Yes. Technical problems such as the scheduling of materials for the next stage of a commissioning task, dealing with an industrial relations problem where there is a laid-down procedural agreement or operational problems with known operational variables, fall into this category.

On the other hand, if the problem or situation is unstructured, then the question is answered No. For example, suppose you have to prepare standard operating procedures, training programmes and fault rectification charts to train a range of operatives on a new chemical plant. The plant is the only one of its kind in Europe and the only other one is in the USA. You have to decide:

(a) What information do I need?
(b) How can I collect it?

The problem is an unstructured one, there is no laid-down procedure for solving it and, perhaps, no previous experience to refer to. At the outset you do not know the answers to (a) or (b), and in this case you would therefore answer No to Question 3. Even if you knew what information was required but were not sure how you could obtain it, you would still answer No because you would need to consult with others.

Question 4
Do I need the acceptance of others to implement my decision?

This question is designed to assess whether you are able to implement the decision effectively without the active co-operation, support or approval of others.

Let us recall the manager, discussed earlier, who had to decide whether or not to introduce trained operator instructors. Suppose he decided to go ahead and introduce these personnel without consulting the men. Almost certainly he would not be able to implement that decision effectively because the men would refuse to participate in the scheme. They might, for example, disagree with the selection and payment of instructors, or argue that there had been a change of duties and responsibilities. Alternatively, if he decided to continue without trained instructors, he might risk having to pay levy to the relevant training board (some boards specify the use of trained instructors as a requirement for exemption from paying levy), and more seriously, if there were an accident, the safety inspectorate might establish that it was the result of a failure to provide adequate instruction, training and information. Thus, Question 4 would be answered Yes. External constraints, such as training board and safety inspectorate requirements, need to be considered when deciding on an appropriate decision-making process, since they must be satisfied if the decision is to be effective.

Consider the manager in Case Study 3 who has to decide which of three trainees from his staff of eight are to work on an overseas assignment which none of them is likely to be keen on because of its location, lack of facilities and lengthy period away from home. If the manager makes an autocratic decision, he is likely to meet opposition from the staff selected because they had not been consulted, and because personal circumstances might make it difficult for them to be away so long.

In a situation like this, Question 4 would be answered Yes.

Take the case of an engineer scheduling materials for stages ahead of a project. He does not need the acceptance of others to implement his decision. He simply works out what is required and instructs the contracting firms of his requirements. Similarly, a headmaster who decides to call a meeting of his staff to discuss a new timetable does not need his staff's approval to implement that decision. He informs them that he intends to hold a staff meeting, in the knowledge that they will comply if possible. In both these cases, Question 4 would be answered No.

Thus, if effective implementation of the decision depends on judgement, creative ability, or the active co-operation of others or the meeting of external criteria, answer Yes.

If others are not involved in executing the decision or the nature of their involvement is compliance rather than acceptance and there are no external criteria to be met, answer No. In this case Question 5 is omitted.

Question 5
Are others likely to accept my decision without being involved in making the decision?

The answer to this question will depend on a number of factors. For example, some leaders, because of their position or status, or because they are regarded as experts, can make autocratic decisions which others accept whereas in other situations this may not be the case.

Thus, a managing director in a small firm which is not unionised is much more likely to have autocratic decisions accepted than one in a large organisation with powerful trade unions to deal with. In the latter case prior consultation or negotiation is often necessary. A metallurgist making technical decisions about operating procedure is able to make a range of decisions which are likely to be accepted because he is seen as the expert. A shop steward on the other hand would almost certainly need to consult with his members before making a decision. Differences in cultural background are also important. Traditionally, for example, Japanese workers are more likely to accept autocratic decisions than British workers. When applying Question 5, the leader must bring to bear his own knowledge and experience of the particular situation. He should ask himself: If I make this decision on my own are others likely to accept it and be committed to its implementation?

Consider the works managers in Case Study 5: they are not likely to accept an autocratic decision by headquarters which adversely affects their transport costs. At the very least they would expect to be consulted beforehand.

Question 6
Do others share the same aims that I want to
achieve in making the decision?

In Case Study 5 the answer to this question would be No,
since there is not a common aim. The man at headquarters
wants to arrive at a minimum cost solution for the company
whereas the works managers want to keep their costs to a
minimum. A marketing manager on the other hand who has
to decide from a number of options a particular advertising
strategy knows that his subordinates are also committed to
the success of the strategy. They may differ about which
option to select but they are all committed to generating a
successful strategy.

Question 6 refers to the extent to which subordinates
would be motivated to pursue a solution to the problem
which matched your aims rather than their own self-interest.

Question 7
Are others, if consulted, likely to accept my decision?

This question is designed to determine whether the leader
should consult or negotiate. It is for the leader to judge on
the basis of his knowledge of the situation whether or not
others are likely to accept his decision on the basis of
consultation.

This question should only be answered Yes if it is
reasonably certain that others will accept the leader's
decision, otherwise the situation could be worsened by the
leader's making a decision which others refuse to accept or
implement. He could then be forced to negotiate under
adverse conditions in which attitudes have hardened.
Particular care needs to be taken when dealing with decisions
about job content, wages or conditions of employment. As a
general rule, these topics are dealt with by negotiation.

Summary

Question 1
*Are decisions likely to differ significantly in their
quality (aim, cost, time)?*

The quality of a decision depends on three factors:

> Achievement of aim
> Cost of implementation
> Time taken to implement decision

If decisions differ significantly in terms of these three
factors — aim, cost, time — answer Yes. Otherwise answer No.

Question 2
Can I make a high quality decision without the aid of others?

This refers to the extent to which you possess the information
or skill required to solve the problem by yourself without the
aid of others. If you answer Yes to this question there is no
need to answer Question 3.

Question 3
Do I know what aid is required and how to obtain it?

This consists of two questions:

> Do I know what aid is required?
> Do I know how to obtain it?

Only if you are able to answer Yes to both questions do you
answer Yes to Question 3.

Question 4
*Do I need the acceptance of others to implement
my decision?*

If others are not involved in executing the decision or the
nature of their involvement is compliance rather than
acceptance and there are no external criteria to satisfy,
answer No, and omit Question 5.
   If the success of the decision depends on judgement,
creative ability or active co-operation of others, answer Yes.

Question 5
*Are others likely to accept my decision without being
involved in making the decision?*

If, by virtue of your position or because you are regarded as
an expert, the decision is likely to be accepted, answer Yes.
If the decision is not likely to be accepted, answer No.

Question 6
*Do others share the same aims that I want to
achieve in making the decision?*

This refers to the extent to which others would be motivated
to pursue a solution to the problem which matched your aims
rather than their own self-interest. If there is a common aim,
answer Yes. If there is a clash of interests, answer No.

Question 7
Are others, if consulted, likely to accept my decision?

Only if you are reasonably certain that others will accept
your decision, based on consultation, should you answer Yes.

7 Analysis of case studies

Let us now analyse each of the six case studies in Chapter 5
by applying the diagnostic questions and then use the
standard network to select decision-making processes.
For ease of reference the network is repeated overleaf.

Before you refer to the analysis below, try analysing each
case study yourself. This will give you practice in using the
diagnostic questions and enable you to compare your results
against those below. This exercise will also enable you to
compare your selection of decision-making processes made in
Chapter 5 against those selected from the analysis.

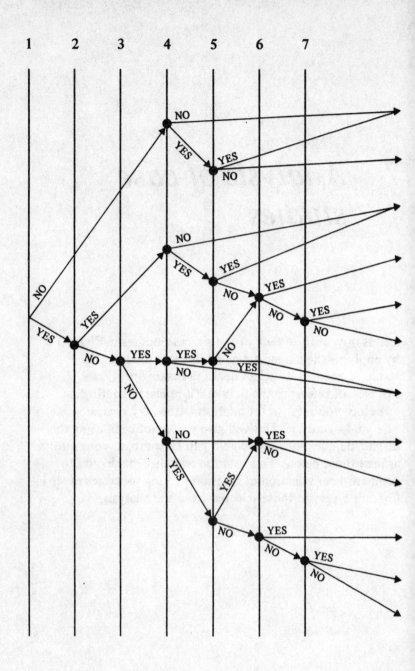

The decision network

Decision-making process	Effective decision
A	*Any decision*
D	Acc_{max}
A or I or C	Q_{max}
C or D	$Q_{max} Acc$
C	$Q_{max} Acc$
N	$Q_{max} Acc$
I or C	$Q_{max} Acc$
C or D	Q_{max}
C	$Q_{max} Acc$
C or D	$Q_{max} Acc$
C	$Q_{max} Acc$
N	$Q_{max} Acc$

KEY:

A	Autocratic
I	Autocratic (information- or skill-seeking)
C	Consultation
N	Negotiation
D	Delegation
Q	Quality
Acc	Acceptability

Diagnostic questions	*Analysis: Case Study 1*

1   We are told that all three contractors are capable
           of doing the work to the required standard and
           that there is little difference in the quoted cost
           or time factors. It is fair to conclude therefore
           that decisions are not likely to differ significantly
           in their quality. It does not matter which
           contractor is selected.

                                 1 = No

2 and 3   Questions 2 and 3 are omitted since they only
           apply when the quality of decisions differs
           significantly — that is, when Question 1 is
           answered Yes.

4   Successful implementation of the decision does
           not depend on the judgement, active co-operation
           or creative ability of others. Acceptance of the
           decision by the salesgirls is not critical to effective
           implementation.

                                 4 = No

5, 6 and 7 Questions 5, 6 and 7 are omitted since 4 = No.

           Thus,   1 = No
                                 4 = No

   Referring to the network, we see that decision-making
process A is indicated. Since neither the quality nor the
acceptability factor is critical, one could literally toss a coin
to make the decision. Thus, in this case one could use A, I,
C or D but it clearly makes sense to use A since the autocratic
approach is less time-consuming and hence less costly than
the other processes.

As a general rule, if more than one decision-making process is capable of generating an effective decision, the one farthest to the left in the last column of the network is selected. Thus, if A, I and C are all acceptable, A is selected on time and cost criteria.

**Diagnostic
questions**   *Analysis: Case Study 2*

1   It is very important that estimates are accurate
                      since if materials are not available at the right
                      time work will be held up. Clearly any delay in
                      commissioning the chemical plant would be
                      costly. Alternatively, if materials arrive too soon
                      they will be lying around idle. Decisions could
                      therefore differ significantly in their quality.

                                          1 = Yes

2   The engineer is familiar with the work in hand
                      and possesses all the necessary information about
                      the materials and equipment required. He there-
                      fore possesses sufficient information to generate
                      a high quality decision.

                                          2 = Yes

3   3 is omitted since the answer to 2 is Yes.

4   The commissioning team are all committed to
                      the aim of commissioning the plant on time.
                      It is therefore in their interest that the engineer
                      generates a high quality decision. In any case,
                      the engineer does not need the acceptance
                      or approval of his commissioning team to
                      implement his decision. He simply works out
                      the highest quality decision and then orders the
                      materials and equipment required.

                                          4 = No

5, 6 and 7   These are omitted since 4 = No.

Thus,   1 = Yes
                               2 = Yes
                               4 = No

The network leads us to A, I or C as appropriate decision-making processes. Since the quality of the decision is critical, the engineer possesses sufficient information to solve it himself without consulting others and there is no acceptability constraint. He could use I or C but in terms of the time and cost involved in making the decision A is the preferred process.

Note: If the engineer did not possess sufficient information to generate a high quality decision (2 = No) but he knew what information was required and where to obtain it (3 = Yes) then one would expect I or C to be used since he would need to obtain the information from others. Applying the analysis 1 = Yes, 2 = No, 3 = Yes, 4 = No to the network, we have confirmation that I or C should be used.

**Diagnostic
questions**   *Analysis: Case Study 3*

1   All of the advisers are experienced personnel
               and each of them is capable of performing the
               task satisfactorily. Therefore, from the training
               manager's point of view it doesn't matter which
               of the advisers are selected. Thus, the quality of
               the decision is not likely to differ significantly.

                            1 = No

2 and 3   These are omitted since 1 = No.

4   The assignment is expected to last about six
               months and is in a remote part of the Middle
               East with poor facilities and a ban on the
               consumption of alcohol. It is unlikely therefore
               that any of the advisers will want to work on
               this assignment. In addition, there may be
               personal reasons which make it inconvenient or
               difficult for some of the advisers to be away
               from home for six months. The manager is
               unlikely therefore to be able to implement
               effectively a decision made in isolation from his
               advisers. He needs their co-operation and
               commitment.

                            4 = Yes

5   It is fairly certain that the advisers would not
               accept the manager's decision without being
               involved in making the decision.

                            5 = No

6 and 7   Since there is no quality requirement (1 = No)
Questions 6 and 7 may be omitted. However, if
you do answer Questions 6 and 7, you will still
arrive at the same answer because of the way
the network is constructed.

Thus,   1 = No
4 = Yes
5 = No

The network indicates D as the appropriate decision-
making process. Since the quality of the decision is not
critical, it does not matter to the leader which decision is
accepted. He is prepared for any three of the advisers to work
on the assignment. He can thus allow the advisers to make
the decision themselves. This process will allow the advisers
to interact with one another in order to resolve any differences
or personal problems and to take full responsibility for
making a decision which is acceptable to them. In this way
the manager is most likely to obtain commitment to the
decision.

**Diagnostic
questions**   *Analysis: Case Study 4*

1   Performance on line 2 will depend to a large
                     extent on the skill of the operatives in rectifying
                     faults and reacting quickly to control panel and
                     VDU cues. Decisions could therefore differ
                     significantly in their quality.

                                     1 = Yes

2   Although you are the project leader, you are not
                     fully informed about the ability of operatives
                     working on line 1. You will need therefore to
                     consult with others in order to obtain the
                     information.

                                     2 = No

3   The project leader knows exactly what
                     information is required and where to obtain it.
                     He requires information about the performance
                     of existing operatives on line 1, the use of tests
                     to determine suitability for training on line 2,
                     etc. He can obtain this information from
                     departmental managers and the training
                     department.

                                     3 = Yes

4   Operatives on line 1 want to transfer to line 2
                     because working conditions are expected to be
                     better and rates of pay higher. Senior operatives
                     expect to be given preference over less senior
                     ones and all operatives on line 1 expect to be
                     given preference over operatives in other
                     departments. If the project leader makes a
                     decision which does not reflect the expectations
                     of the men, he is likely to meet strong opposition

from them and the union concerned. Clearly then, acceptability of the decision is a critical factor.

4 = Yes

5 Since rates of pay and working conditions are involved, there is little chance that any decision would be accepted without the involvement of the men or their union.

5 = No

6 The leader wants to select and transfer only the best operatives to line 2 in order to ensure that the line operates at maximum efficiency. The men on the other hand are motivated primarily from self-interest since they are more concerned with pay and improved working conditions. There is clearly therefore a clash of interests.

6 = No

7 Since working conditions and rates of pay are involved the men are unlikely to accept the leader's decision, even if they are consulted beforehand.

7 = No

Thus,

1 = Yes
2 = No
3 = Yes
4 = Yes
5 = No
6 = No
7 = No.

According to the network, N is the decision-making process most likely to generate an effective decision. Since the men

are not likely to accept a decision by the project leader
(5 = No) without their involvement, some degree of
participation is necessary. This rules out the use of A or I.
There is no common aim (6 = No) so the decision-making
process cannot be delegated. In other words, D is ruled out.
Since they are unlikely to accept the leader's decision based
on consultation (7 = No), C is ruled out, which leaves N.

The men will clearly want to generate solutions which
match their own aims rather than those of the leader. Thus
for the leader to consult (C) and ask for suggested solutions
which he may then reject because they fail to meet his aims
is likely to worsen matters. Therefore, unless the leader is
fairly confident that the men are likely to accept his decision
based on consultation, he should negotiate a solution which
is acceptable to all parties.

This is, in fact, a typical example of the type of problem
faced by management today, in dealing with the introduction
of new technology which improves efficiency of operation
but which often results in redundancy or change in working
conditions. Experience is beginning to show that provision of
information, discussion and negotiation at an early stage can
avoid a great deal of the disruption which partial knowledge
and rumour have caused in the past.

**Diagnostic
questions**   *Analysis: Case Study 5*

1   This case has already been dealt with at some
           length in Chapter 6 when it was established that
           transport costs could vary between £82,000 and
           £90,000. Decisions are therefore likely to differ
           significantly in their quality.

                              1 = Yes

2   The head office manager knows the warehouse
           demands, transport costs and factory outputs.
           He thus possesses all of the information required
           to generate a high quality decision.

                              2 = Yes

3   This question is omitted since 2 = Yes.

4   We are told that the pattern of distribution is
           changed from time to time as a result of
           complaints from factory and warehouse
           managers. This is understandable since works
           costs can be adversely affected by implemen-
           tation of the minimum cost solution worked
           out in Chapter 6.

                              4 = Yes

5   The works managers are not likely to accept an
           autocratic decision by headquarters which
           adversely affects their transport costs. At the
           very least they would expect to be consulted.

                              5 = No

6   There obviously is no common aim. Headquarters
             want a solution which keeps costs to a minimum
             overall whereas the works managers want to
             keep their costs to a minimum, and yet, as we
             saw in Chapter 6, the minimum solution overall
             is not the minimum cost solution for the
             individual works.

                                6 = No

7   It is virtually certain that the works managers
             will accept the decision providing they have been
             consulted beforehand.

                                7 = Yes

             Thus,   1 = Yes
                                2 = Yes
                                4 = Yes
                                5 = No
                                6 = No
                                7 = Yes

   The network indicates C as the appropriate decision-
making process. In this case it is important to keep overall
costs to a minimum since this clearly affects the profitability
of the company. Consultation is therefore the most
appropriate process to use since this allows the leader to
inform the managers of the facts and to discuss the situation
with them, while enabling him to make the final decision.

**Diagnostic
questions**   *Analysis: Case Study 6*

1   Since the information is used to make important
               quality control and assurance decisions the
               quality of the decisions could differ significantly.

                              1 = Yes

2   We are told that the trouble-shooter possesses
               information on the different terminology being
               used but not on local practices for recording
               information. He does not therefore possess
               sufficient information to generate a high quality
               decision.

                              2 = No

3   He knows what information is required and that
               he can obtain it from the works quality control
               staff.

                              3 = Yes

4   We are told that successful implementation of a
               common recording system will require the active
               co-operation and commitment of the works
               quality control staff.

                              4 = Yes

5   Since the trouble-shooter is from division, works
               staff are unlikely to accept his decision without
               their involvement in the making of the decision,
               especially since they may resent divisional
               interference in works operating procedure.

                              5 = No

6   Both division and works would benefit from a standardised system, so it is in the interests of all parties to improve the existing system.

6 = Yes

7   Since there is a common aim and they all stand to benefit from an improved system, works staff are likely to accept the trouble-shooter's recommendation, provided they have been fully consulted.

	7 = Yes
Thus,	1 = Yes
	2 = No
	3 = Yes
	4 = Yes
	5 = No
	6 = Yes
	7 = Yes

From the network we have C or D as appropriate processes. Since the works quality control staff are all committed to the aim of improving the existing system, it can be taken that they would do their best to generate a high quality decision and the use of D would allow differences between works staff to be discussed and resolved. Also a group-generated solution is much more likely to achieve maximum acceptability and commitment.

It is for the leader to judge which process to use. If he has any doubt about the group's ability to generate a high quality decision or feels that inter-works rivalry is such that the use of D is likely to damage the quality of the decision, then he should use C.

8 Summary

Factors influencing the effectiveness of decisions

The key factors in any effective decision are the *quality* of the decision (aim, cost and time) and its *acceptability* to others. The effective decision (ED) in a particular situation depends on the relative importance of the quality and acceptability factors. There are four cases to consider. These are:

$$ED = Q_{max}Acc$$
$$ED = Q_{max}$$
$$ED = Acc_{max}$$
$$ED = any\ decision$$

Decision-making processes

We have identified five decision-making processes. These are:

A = Autocratic
I = Autocratic information- or skill-seeking
C = Consultation
N = Negotiation
D = Delegation

Diagnostic questions

There are seven diagnostic questions.
These are:

1. Are decisions likely to differ significantly in their quality?
2. Can I make a high quality decision without the aid of others?
3. Do I know what aid is required and how to obtain it?
4. Do I need the acceptance of others to implement my decision?
5. Are others likely to accept my decision without being involved in making the decision?
6. Do others share the same aims that I want to achieve in making the decision?
7. Are others, if consulted, likely to accept my decision?

9 Exercises

The following exercises are in the form of additional case studies. To obtain the maximum benefit readers should carry out their own analysis and selection of decision-making process before referring to the solutions given in the text.

MARKETING A COMPETITIVE PRODUCT

You are the managing director and chairman of the board of a firm manufacturing a single product in a highly competitive market. You have three competitors, and over the past twelve months your sales have fluctuated between 16,400 and 25,000 units per month. The market is very price-sensitive and two of your competitors have recently dropped their prices to slightly below yours. The third competitor is selling at a slightly higher price than you.

You have reason to believe that your competitors are substantially increasing their marketing expenditure, and one has invested in new research and development laboratories. There has been a 10 per cent growth in the total market over the past two years and you intuitively expect the growth to continue. One of your competitors has invested in new plant and equipment which will increase output and is expected to increase productivity and lower production costs.

Your board has to decide:

1. Selling price
2. Marketing expenditure
3. Research and development expenditure
4. Investment policy — new plant and equipment

Diagnostic questions	*Analysis*
1 = Yes	Clearly these decisions are crucial to the success of the firm. They represent corporate decisions which can either lead to profit or plunge the firm into decline.
2 = No	Your expectation of continued growth is based on past experience and your 'feeling for the situation'. There is obviously a need for more objective information. You also need, for example, information on capital expenditure costs.
3 = Yes	You know what information is required and how to obtain it: Market survey Capital expenditure appraisal Sensitivity analysis (What happens if I increase the selling price by x and decrease marketing expenditure by y?)
4 = Yes	You will need the support and commitment of the board and you must take account of shareholders' views.
5 = No	The board, and possibly senior management and shareholders, would expect to be involved.
6 = Yes	All are committed to the aim of maximising profitability and improving long-term survival prospects.
7 = Yes	It is almost certain that others will accept the decision, provided adequate consultation has been carried out.

Decision-making process: consultation

In this case, C would be the appropriate decision-making process since this would allow the board to commission teams, individuals or consultants to carry out a market survey, do a capital expenditure appraisal or a sensitivity analysis. This and other information gathered as a result of broadly-based consultations would then form the basis for the board's decisions.

QUALITY CONTROL

You are a quality control manager in charge of a multi-discipline team. For some time customers have been complaining about the surface quality of one of your products. So far you have not been able to identify the causes of the problem from your discussions with plant personnel responsible for the manufacture of this product. You are particularly concerned about this case because one of your biggest customers is involved and there is growing competition from foreign manufacturers who are trying hard to break into the market. All of your team are highly motivated individuals and are just as concerned about this problem as you.

Diagnostic questions	*Analysis*
1 = Yes	You could lose an important customer.
2 = No	You do not know the cause of the problem.
3 = No	You know how to obtain the information but you do not know exactly what information is required.
4 = No	This is a compliance rather than an acceptance situation.
5 = Yes	As in 4.
6 = Yes	All of your team want to solve this problem.

Decision-making process: consultation or delegation

Since your team are highly motivated individuals, all committed to solving this problem, you could delegate it to them to solve in the knowledge that they would do their best to generate high quality decisions. In practice, you would probably ask one or two members of the team to do an investigation into the causes of the problem and make recommendations, and then consult with the whole team before making a decision.

TECHNICAL PROBLEM

You are an engineer in charge of a small chemical plant.
You have to decide which acid tank lining to choose from
six materials. You supervise forty subordinates including
six chemists and two metallurgists. You know the process
variables such as pressure, temperature and acid strength
for the various process operations. You do not know the
mechanical, electrical or corrosion characteristics of all of
the six materials under consideration but you do know
where the information can be obtained. A quick decision is
essential because it is hoped to commission the new vessels
in a few weeks. However, great care is needed in selecting
the material because serious operational problems have
been caused in the past due to lining corrosion and
collapse.

**Diagnostic
questions**   *Analysis*

1 = Yes   Selection of the correct material is essential since
                 serious operational problems could result from
                 the use of an inferior material.

2 = No   You do not know the mechanical, electrical or
                 corrosion characteristics of the six materials.

3 = Yes   This information can be obtained from the
                 manufacturers.

4 = No   You could implement your decision without
                 consulting with your subordinates.

**Decision-making process: autocratic information-seeking
or consultation**

Since speed is essential and acceptability is not a problem,
the I process is the one most likely to be used. You know
what information is required, so you simply ask for it and
evaluate it before making your decision. However, if in doubt,
you may, of course, consult with your subordinates.

PERSONNEL

You are the director of a small organisation. For some
time you have been dissatisfied with the management
structure, which you believe is adversely affecting
efficiency. You have recently had a job evaluation exercise
carried out by a firm of consultants and you would like to
implement some of their recommendations.

Unfortunately the proposed changes would mean a
number of job losses and also a change of duties for the
remainder of the management team. All of your managers
are members of a trade union and for some time there has
been speculation and some alarm expressed about the
evaluation exercise, especially since your managers had not
been consulted beforehand. You realise that your
management team feel threatened and that there could be
problems in implementing the proposals.

Diagnostic questions	*Analysis*
1 = Yes	Decisions could influence the operating efficiency of the organisation.
2 = Yes	You possess the report of the consultants plus your own knowledge and experience of the situation.
4 = Yes	Job losses and change of duties are involved.
5 = No	Since their jobs are at stake they are unlikely to accept any decision without being involved.
6 = No	There is obviously a clash of interests since you want to introduce redundancy and change of duties whereas the managers want to keep their jobs.
7 = No	Again, since job losses and change of duties are involved managers may still object to a decision made on the basis of consultation only.

Decision-making process: negotiation

In practice job losses and change of duties are normally dealt with by negotiation.

NEW PRODUCT LAUNCH

You are a marketing manager in charge of a regional team. You have decided to launch a new technical product by means of area conferences. The product has been costly to develop and it is vital that the conferences are a success especially since you operate in a highly competitive market.

You have to decide on the venue in each area, the conference structure, whom to invite and who is to address the conferences. Each member of your team possesses detailed information about his own area and expects to be asked to address the conference. However, you realise that although all members of your team are effective in a face-to-face selling situation some of them are not so good as lecturers.

Diagnostic questions	*Analysis*
1 = Yes	The product has been costly to develop and you operate in a highly competitive market.
2 = No	You do not possess detailed knowledge of the areas.
3 = Yes	The information can be obtained from your area manager.
4 = Yes	The commitment of area staff is vital to successful implementation.
5 = No	Each of the area managers is likely to be very upset if he is not involved in this matter.
6 = Yes/No	In part they do share the same aims since they all want the conference to succeed, but you do not want all of your area managers to present the material because they are not all competent to do so. On balance therefore the answer is probably No.
7 = Yes	

Decision-making process: consultation

You can only obtain the information you require from the area managers. At the same time process C leaves you free to make the final decision as to who is to address the conferences. During the consultative period you could, for example, argue that it would be better to use just one person to address the conferences in order to achieve a consistent approach and reduce costs.

Appendix
Elimination of decision-making processes

The decision network is based on ten rules. Before explaining them, some points of clarification are required about the construction and use of the network.

Some questions may not apply to a particular problem situation. Thus, questions 2 and 3 only apply if question 1 is answered Yes. Similarly, questions 6 and 7 do not apply if question 1 is answered No and question 5 is answered Yes. That is, the quality factor is not critical and 'others are likely to accept the leader's decision without being involved in making the decision'. There is, therefore, no need to answer questions 6 and 7. However, even if these questions are answered, the network is constructed in such a way that it will by-pass questions which do not apply to a particular problem situation.

For example, from the network, when question 1 is answered No, the network path by-passes questions 2 and 3 and moves directly to question 4. Suppose a problem situation is analysed as follows:

$$1 = \text{Yes}$$
$$2 = \text{Yes}$$
$$3 = \text{Yes}$$
$$4 = \text{No}$$
$$5 = \text{Yes}$$
$$6 = \text{Yes}$$
$$7 = \text{Yes}$$

From the network it can be seen that the path goes directly from question 2 to question 4. This is because the leader is able to generate high quality decisions without the aid of others (2 = Yes): thus, question 3 does not apply. Similarly the path goes from question 4 directly to decision-making processes A, I and C, by-passing questions 5, 6 and 7 because, in this case, they do not apply. Thus, although the questions have been answered, they are by-passed when the analysis is applied to the network.

From an examination of the rules it can be seen that some questions are answered Yes and No. This is because in certain situations these questions may be answered either Yes or No without affecting the choice of decision-making process.

For example, from the network it can be seen that when

$$\begin{array}{ccc} 1 = \text{No} & & 1 = \text{No} \\ & \text{or} & 4 = \text{Yes} \\ 4 = \text{No} & & 5 = \text{Yes} \end{array}$$

the decision-making process in both cases is A. This represents rule 1. The rule is therefore fixed by questions 1 and 5 since the answer to question 4 may be either Yes or No without affecting the choice of DMP. In the first problem situation 1 = No, 4 = No, question 5 must clearly be Yes since question 4 is No. However, since it is not a branching question (in this case, that is), it can only be answered Yes and is omitted. The network is constructed to by-pass questions which are implied by the answers to previous questions. Thus, both problem situations are variations of a general problem situation which may be expressed as:

$$1 = \text{No}$$
$$4 = \text{Yes/No}$$
$$5 = \text{Yes}$$

Let us take another example. From the network, it can be seen that when:

$$
\begin{array}{ll}
1 = \text{Yes} & \\
2 = \text{Yes} & \quad 1 = \text{Yes} \\
4 = \text{Yes} \quad \text{or} & \quad 2 = \text{Yes} \\
5 = \text{Yes} & \quad 4 = \text{No}
\end{array}
$$

The DMPs in both cases are A, I or C.
This represents rule 3 which is fixed by questions:

$$1 = \text{Yes}$$
$$2 = \text{Yes}$$
$$5 = \text{Yes}$$

In the second problem situation 1 = Yes, 2 = Yes and 4 = No, question 5 is omitted because it is implied by the answer to question 4 being No. That is, when question 4 is No, question 5 must be Yes. Thus, both specific problem situations are variations of a general problem situation which may be expressed as:

$$1 = \text{Yes}$$
$$2 = \text{Yes}$$
$$4 = \text{Yes/No}$$
$$5 = \text{Yes}$$

If you turn to rule 6 (see page 86) it will be seen that there are three variations of the general problem situation. In one of these, question 7 is answered Yes, whereas in the other two variations question 7 is omitted. This is because in one of the specific problem situations question 5 is answered Yes: it follows, therefore, that question 7 must be answered Yes. Similarly with the second variation, question 4 is answered

No, so question 7 must again be Yes. All three are therefore
variations of a general problem type.

The network is constructed to by-pass questions which do
not apply and questions to which the answers are implied
from the answers to previous questions. Thus, taking one of
the variations of rule 6 as an example:

$$1 = \text{Yes}$$
$$2 = \text{No}$$
$$3 = \text{No}$$
$$4 = \text{Yes}$$
$$5 = \text{Yes}$$
$$6 = \text{No}$$

it can be seen that the network path goes directly from
question 6 to DMP C, by-passing question 7 which is implied
by the Yes answer to question 5.

Let us now consider each of the ten rules in turn.

Rule 1
When

$$1 = No$$
$$4 = Yes/No$$
$$5 = Yes$$

The decision-making process is A

This rule includes problem situations in which there are no quality or acceptability requirements (1 = No and 5 = Yes). In situations such as these, questions 2, 3, 6 and 7 do not apply. Since there are no quality or acceptability requirements any DMP will generate an effective decision: it therefore makes sense to use the A process since this is the least time-consuming and hence least costly way of making the decision. There is no point in using participative processes which are likely to slow down the making of the decision.

Rule 1 contains problem situations which may be analysed as:

$$1 = No \qquad 1 = No$$
$$4 = No \quad or \quad 4 = Yes$$
$$5 = Yes$$

In both cases, the A decision-making process is the most appropriate one to use.

Thus, in problem situations analysed as follows:

$$1 = No$$
$$4 = Yes/No$$
$$5 = Yes$$

DMP is A = Rule 1

Rule 2
   When

$$1 = No$$
$$4 = Yes$$
$$5 = No$$

The decision-making process is D
When decisions are not likely to differ significantly in their
quality (1 = No) but the acceptability factor is critical
(4 = Yes and 5 = No), the aim is to generate a decision which
is most acceptable to others (Acc_{max}). Because the quality
factor is not critical the leader can accept any decision which
is acceptable to others. The problem should therefore be
delegated to allow differences to be reconciled and also to
gain maximum commitment to the decision. In general,
problem situations with no quality requirement but with an
acceptability problem should be delegated since this increases
the chances of generating an Acc_{max} decision.

   Thus, in problem situations analysed as follows:

$$1 = No$$
$$4 = Yes$$
$$5 = No$$

DMP is D = Rule 2

Rule 3
When

$$1 = Yes$$
$$2 = Yes$$
$$4 = Yes/No$$
$$5 = Yes$$

The decision-making process is A, I, or C

Since the quality factor is important (1 = Yes), the leader possesses sufficient information to make a high quality decision alone (2 = Yes) and there is no acceptability problem (5 = Yes), the A process would normally be used. However, since the quality factor is important the leader may decide to seek more information, I, or consult, C, in order to optimise his chances of generating a Q_{max} decision. Thus, the use of A, I or C is likely to generate an effective decision and illustrates the fact that a range of decision-making processes can sometimes be used.

Problem situations of this type may be analysed as:

$$1 = Yes \quad\quad 1 = Yes$$
$$2 = Yes \quad or \quad 2 = Yes$$
$$4 = Yes \quad\quad 4 = No$$
$$5 = Yes$$

Thus, in general, in problem situations analysed as follows:

$$1 = Yes$$
$$2 = Yes$$
$$4 = Yes/No$$
$$5 = Yes$$

DMP is A, I or C = Rule 3

Rule 4
   When

$$
\begin{aligned}
1 &= \text{Yes}\\
2 &= \text{Yes}\\
4 &= \text{Yes}\\
5 &= \text{No}\\
6 &= \text{No}\\
7 &= \text{Yes}
\end{aligned}
$$

The decision-making process is C
Since decisions are likely to differ significantly in their
quality (1 = Yes) and others are not likely to accept the
decision without being involved in making it (5 = No) the A
and I processes are ruled out. There is no common aim
(6 = No) so the leader must retain control of the decision-
making process, otherwise a decision may be made which
reflects others' self-interests rather than the leader's aim.
Thus, D is ruled out. This leaves C or N as possibilities but as
others, if consulted, are likely to accept the decision (7 = Yes)
there is no need to negotiate. This leaves C as the DMP most
likely to generate a $Q_{max} Acc$ decision.
   Thus, in problem situations analysed as follows:

$$
\begin{aligned}
1 &= \text{Yes}\\
2 &= \text{Yes}\\
4 &= \text{Yes}\\
5 &= \text{No}\\
6 &= \text{No}\\
7 &= \text{Yes}
\end{aligned}
$$

DMP is C = Rule 4

Rule 5
When

$$1 = Yes$$
$$2 = Yes$$
$$4 = Yes$$
$$5 = No$$
$$6 = Yes$$

The decision-making process is C or D

Since both quality and acceptability factors are important
(1 = Yes and 5 = No) the aim is to generate the highest
quality decision that is acceptable to others ($Q_{max} Acc$) thus
A and I are ruled out. Negotiation is not necessary since
there is a common aim (C = Yes). This leaves C or D as
possible processes. If the leader is confident that others
possess sufficient skill and knowledge to generate a high
quality decision, it makes sense to use the D process since
this is most likely to generate a $Q_{max} Acc$ decision. On the
other hand, if the leader has doubts about others' ability to
generate high quality decisions the C process should be used.

Thus, in problem situations analysed as follows:

$$1 = Yes$$
$$2 = Yes$$
$$4 = Yes$$
$$5 = No$$
$$6 = Yes$$

DMP is C or D = Rule 5

Rule 6
   When

1 = Yes	5 = Yes/No
2 = No	6 = No
3 = No	7 = Yes
4 = Yes/No	

The decision-making process is C

The quality of the decision is important (1 = Yes). The leader does not possess sufficient information to make a high quality decision (2 = No) and doesn't know what information is needed nor how to obtain it (3 = No). The A and I processes are therefore ruled out. Since there is no common aim (6 = No) the decision cannot be left to others, which rules out D. Negotiation is also ruled out (7 = Yes) which leaves C. With problem situations of this kind, wide-ranging consultation is necessary to determine what information is needed and how it can be obtained.

   Problems of this type may be analysed as:

1 = Yes	1 = Yes	1 = Yes
2 = No	2 = No	2 = No
3 = No	3 = No	3 = No
4 = Yes or	4 = Yes or	4 = No
5 = Yes	5 = No	6 = No
6 = No	6 = No	
	7 = Yes	

Thus, in general, in problem situations analysed as follows:

1 = Yes	5 = Yes/No
2 = No	6 = No
3 = No	7 = Yes
4 = Yes/No	

DMP is C = Rule 6

Rule 7
When

$$
\begin{aligned}
1 &= \text{Yes} \\
2 &= \text{No} \\
3 &= \text{No} \\
4 &= \text{Yes/No} \\
5 &= \text{Yes/No} \\
6 &= \text{Yes}
\end{aligned}
$$

The decision-making process is C or D

Problem situations of this type are the same as for rule 6 except that in this case there is a common aim (6 = Yes). As for rule 6, the A and I processes are ruled out and since there is a common aim N is also eliminated which leaves C or D. As for rule 6, the leader needs to consult widely in order to establish what information is needed and how it may be obtained (2 and 3 = No). In this case, however, since there is a common aim (6 = Yes) the leader can delegate it to others if he feels that they are competent to generate high quality decisions. If not, he should use C.

Problems of this type may be analysed as follows:

1 = Yes		1 = Yes		1 = Yes
2 = No		2 = No		2 = No
3 = No	or	3 = No	or	3 = No
4 = Yes		4 = Yes		4 = No
5 = Yes		5 = No		6 = Yes
6 = Yes		6 = Yes		

Thus, in general, in problem situations analysed as follows:

$$
\begin{aligned}
1 &= \text{Yes} \\
2 &= \text{No} \\
3 &= \text{No} \\
4 &= \text{Yes/No} \\
5 &= \text{Yes/No} \\
6 &= \text{Yes}
\end{aligned}
$$

DMP is C or D = Rule 7

Rule 8
When

$$1 = \text{Yes}$$
$$2 = \text{No}$$
$$3 = \text{Yes}$$
$$4 = \text{Yes}$$
$$5 = \text{Yes}$$

The decision-making process is I or C

The quality factor is important (1 = Yes) but the leader does not possess sufficient information to generate a high quality decision. This rules out the use of the A process. Since there is no acceptability problem (5 = Yes) and the leader knows what information is required and how to obtain it (3 = Yes) the I process would normally be used. However, if the leader considers that sharing the problem with others is likely to generate a higher quality decision, he should use the C process.

Thus, in problem situations analysed as follows:

$$1 = \text{Yes}$$
$$2 = \text{No}$$
$$3 = \text{Yes}$$
$$4 = \text{Yes}$$
$$5 = \text{Yes}$$

DMP is I or C = Rule 8

Rule 9
  When

$$1 = Yes$$
$$2 = No$$
$$3 = Yes$$
$$4 = Yes$$
$$5 = No$$
$$6 = Yes$$

The decision-making process is C or D

Problem situations of this type are similar to rule 7 except that in this case the leader knows what information is needed and how to obtain it (3 = Yes). The A, I and N processes are ruled out because 2 = No, 5 = No and 6 = Yes, which leaves C or D. If time is a critical factor or the leader has doubts about others' ability to generate high quality decisions, the C process should be used, otherwise the D process should be used since it is likely to generate greater commitment to the decision.

  Thus, in problem situations analysed as follows:

$$1 = Yes$$
$$2 = No$$
$$3 = Yes$$
$$4 = Yes$$
$$5 = No$$
$$6 = Yes$$

DMP is C or D = Rule 9

Rule 10
When

1 = Yes
2 = Yes/No
3 = Yes/No
4 = Yes
5 = No
6 = No
7 = No

The decision-making process is N
Decisions are likely to differ significantly in their quality
(1 = Yes). Since others are not likely to accept the decision
without being involved in making it (5 = No) and there is no
common aim (6 = No) A, I and D are ruled out. Moreover,
since the decision is not likely to be accepted on the basis of
consultation, (7 = No) the C process is ruled out. This leaves
negotiation as the appropriate decision-making process to use.
Problems of this type may be analysed as:

1 = Yes		1 = Yes		1 = Yes
2 = Yes		2 = No		2 = No
4 = Yes		3 = Yes		3 = No
5 = No	or	4 = Yes	or	4 = Yes
6 = No		5 = No		5 = No
7 = No		6 = No		6 = No
		7 = No		7 = No

Thus, in general, in problem situations analysed as follows:

1 = Yes
2 = Yes/No
3 = Yes/No
4 = Yes
5 = No
6 = No
7 = No

DMP is N = Rule 10